A Gift For

Ricardo

♡ Feb.
2013

From

Yvonne

Our 1st Valentine's Day ♡

Forever Love

50 SECRETS FROM 50 COUPLES MARRIED 50 YEARS... and *Still* in Love

TODD HAFER

summerside
PRESS

Summerside Press™
Minneapolis, MN 55378
SummersidePress.com

Forever Love
© 2012 by Todd Hafer

ISBN 978-1-60936-199-0

Stock or custom editions of Summerside Press titles may be purchased in bulk for educational, business, ministry, fundraising, or sales promotional use. For information, please email specialmarkets@summersidepress.com.

Cover and interior design by Greg Jackson | Thinkpen Design

Cover Image © 2012 Shutterstock

Summerside Press is an inspirational publisher offering fresh, irresistible books to uplift the heart and engage the mind.

Printed in China

To all of the couples and their
families who shared their love stories.

And to a certain smashing blonde, with
hopes and prayers that she will be able to
put up with the author for 50 years.

Contents

*Y*ou know you're in love when
you can't fall asleep
because reality is finally better
than your dreams.

DR. SEUSS

If I speak in the tongues of mortals and of angels, but do not
have love, I am a noisy gong or a clanging cymbal.
And if I have prophetic powers, and understand all mysteries
and all knowledge, and if I have all faith, so as to remove
mountains, but do not have love, I am nothing.
If I give away all my possessions, and if I hand over my body
so that I may boast, but do not have love, I gain nothing.
Love is patient; love is kind;
love is not envious or boastful
or arrogant or rude.
It does not insist on its own way;
it is not irritable or resentful;
it does not rejoice in wrongdoing,
but rejoices in truth.
It bears all things, believes all things,
hopes all things, endures all things.
Love never ends. . . .
And now faith, hope, and love abide, these three;
and the greatest of these is love.

I CORINTHIANS 13:1–8, 13 NRSV

Preface

I spent days trying to write a proper preamble for this book. After more than a dozen years of interviewing, researching, and, finally, writing more than 50 stories, how hard could it be to type a few words of introduction?

As it turns out, stupid-hard.

Then I thought of my lone surviving grandparent, 96-year-old Esther Hafer, whose long, long marriage to my Grandpa Jay sparked the idea for this book many years ago. I called her on the phone. (Grandma does not email. Grandma does not text. And don't even think about asking her to Tweet.) I asked if she was game for a small assignment.

A few days later (well ahead of my suggested deadline), I received the following handwritten piece.

Thanks, Grandma. The check's in the mail. Really.

TODD HAFER (author and grateful grandson)

Introduction

Marriage is a great institution that God has given to His people. It can fulfill every girl's dream and every man's hopes. Marriage is two minds, two hearts, and two bodies— united to face the world and whatever the future holds.

In a loving marriage, a wife and a husband find the strength to inspire, comfort, help, and encourage one another. They enjoy each other; they enjoy *life*.

How do I know all of this? I lived it for 72 years, with my beloved Jay Hafer. I am honored and proud that Jay and I are part of my grandson's book—along with the other couples who have been blessed with Golden Anniversaries— and beyond.

ESTHER HAFER
Spring, 2012

1

Forget about that whole 50/50 thing.

Barb and Tim Strawberry

MARRIED OCTOBER 29, 1952

"I've heard it said that marriage is a fifty-fifty proposition," Tim Strawberry growls. "Well, where I went to high school, fifty percent was a failing grade. And you couldn't find some other joker who also got a fifty, add his score to yours, and then start crowing, 'Hey, look at me! I got a hundred percent!'"

The Strawberrys sometimes speak to young couples, and they always encourage their audience to avoid saying things like, "I'm carrying my share of the load; how 'bout you?"

"A husband and a wife must be willing to carry the *whole* load when necessary," Barb asserts. "That's what it's gonna take sometimes, so that needs to be your attitude. I don't recall Jesus talking about going the extra hundred yards!"

Tim adds, "You never know when one of you is going to be sick, injured, down in the dumps, or just plain worn ragged. At times like that, it's such a blessing if your partner can step in and say, 'Rest easy, darlin'. I got this.'"

Barb and Tim say that being willing to serve each other, in ways large and small, has been a hallmark of their long and happy marriage.

"We don't demand that we meet each other halfway," Barb notes. "We both strive to be willing to go the *whole* way. Give our complete effort. If either of us sees something that needs to be done, we just up and do it. And I'll tell you something: Effort isn't a pain in the neck when it's flowing from the love that is in your heart."

"We've always been willing to go the extra mile for each other," Tim concludes, "and I think that's why we're miles ahead of most of the other couples we know."

Bear one another's burdens, and
thereby fulfill the law of Christ.

GALATIANS 6:2 NASB

*W*here love is concerned,
too much is not enough.

PIERRE DE BEAUMARCHAIS

2

Be the first to say "I'm sorry."

Shelly and Cal Starr
MARRIED DECEMBER 24, 1956

"It was agonizing, sitting there in a tense house, waiting for the apology that I thought was owed to me," Cal Starr recalls. "That's how I dealt with marital conflict for the first couple of years with Shelly. After a while, I had to ask myself, 'Exactly how long do you want to sit here and be stubborn—feeling tense and hurt and miserable?'"

As Cal ultimately learned, waiting for an apology or an admission of wrong that we think is owed to us can be some of the loneliest and most frustrating waiting there is.

"The sad thing is," Shelly explains, "Cal would be downstairs, sitting in his chair, miserable, while he was waiting for me to apologize. Meanwhile,

I'd be up in the bedroom, staring at the ceiling and waiting for *his* apology. I honestly don't remember who first broke the impasse, but once that happened, it was like we had broken free from heavy chains. Now, it's practically a race between us to see who apologizes first."

"It's not important to determine who is more wrong, or who offended whom first," Cal agrees. "The important thing is that both of us want to mend the damage that's been done. Both of us want to give the heavenly gift of forgiveness. Both of us want to make peace. The sooner you get past all that stupid finger-pointing, the sooner you'll get to the making up! And maybe even making out, too!"

"Cal!" Shelly scolds.

Cal shrugs his shoulders. "I'm *so* sorry," he says.

> *Be completely humble and gentle;*
> *be patient, bearing with one another in love.*

EPHESIANS 4:2

*L*ove is an act of endless forgiveness,
a tender look which becomes a habit.

PETER USTINOV

3

Embrace the magic of the intangible.

"Whatever does she see in *him*?"

"I never pictured a guy like him with a girl like *her*."

"Have you ever seen a couple as odd as those two!?"

"I give that couple two or three years, *tops*."

"Maybe opposites attract—but NOT that kind of opposite!"

How many times have you heard gossip like this? Or maybe a friend posed the same question to you about one of your romantic choices. Some people look at things like differences in age, race, economic background, or personality type, and then cast doubts on a relationship's viability. But couples like the Swintons have learned that sometimes it's the things that aren't immediately obvious—the intangibles—that make for an enduring relationship.

"I don't know how to explain it," Sarah says, "but there's just something about Reggie. Music always sounds better when we're together."

Reggie agrees.

"When she's around," he smiles, "food tastes better, the wind is kinder, sunsets are more beautiful…heck, everything is just plain better."

There is a place, of course, for lists and formulas and criteria when it comes to starting and building a relationship. But the Swintons have learned that intangible magic can have a profound impact on the very tangible institution of marriage.

As Sarah puts it, "Sometimes the heart knows things that the brain just cannot put into words. I thank God that Reggie and I have a soul connection, because that's the strongest kind of connection there is."

*May your fountain be blessed, and may
you rejoice in the wife of your youth…may
you ever be intoxicated with her love.*

PROVERBS 5:18-19

*W*hatever our souls are made of,
his and mine are the same.

EMILY BRONTË

4

In love, the little things count—because they are signs of the big things.

Brandon and Kelly Davis
MARRIED JANUARY 1, 1955

Kelly Davis has a simple answer to those who ask what first attracted her to husband Brandon.

"Why him?" she smiles, "He smelled the best."

Kelly's answer might seem flippant, but it's not. She notes, "I figured if a guy took the trouble to smell better than all the rest of 'em, he'd probably be committed to being outstanding in other areas as well. And that's proven to be the case. For example, in addition to smelling great, he has one humdinger of a kiss!"

For his part, Brandon notes, "The whole reason I was so diligent about being a good-smelling gent was so that I could attract someone like Kelly. And you know what? It worked!"

It's still working, five and a half decades later. This couple, who were married on a New Year's Day in Brattleboro, Vermont, say they still find new things, large and small, that keep their love going strong.

"It was true then, and it's true now," Kelly says: "God's blessings come in *lots* of sizes."

"And smells, too," Brandon adds. "Don't forget that!"

There are three things that are
too amazing for me,
four that I do not understand:
the way of an eagle in the sky,
the way of a snake on a rock,
the way of a ship on the high seas,
and the way of a man with a young woman.

PROVERBS 30:18–19

*L*ove is what makes two people sit
in the middle of a bench when there's
plenty of room at both ends.

UNKNOWN

5

*Take heart—
love is still
undefeated.*

John and Nellie Wooden
MARRIED AUGUST 8, 1932

Just a few days before he was to be married to his beloved Nellie Riley, 21-year-old John Wooden lost his life savings ($909.05) due to a bank failure. Only a loan from a friend allowed John and his high school sweetheart—the only girl he ever kissed romantically—to go through with their wedding. They celebrated their honeymoon by attending a Mills Brothers concert.

Then the Woodens established a humble household. John played small-time professional basketball while also teaching high school classes and coaching basketball to make ends meet. The couple lived quietly for a decade—until World War II—when John left home to fight for his country. He returned from military service only to see the bank foreclose on their home.

Undaunted, he took on multiple jobs at Indiana State University. John served as ISU's athletic director, head basketball coach, and head baseball coach. He also taught several classes and completed his Masters thesis.

Three years later, Coach Wooden headed west and took a job at UCLA, where he became a legend. He led the Bruins to ten national basketball championships, including seven in a row. Nellie was a constant source of support and love, and she took the lead in caring for the couple's two children during the hectic basketball seasons. He called her "the greatest co-coach, working alongside me."

"Folks think Nellie and I had a perfect marriage," the coach was fond of saying, "but it was because we worked at it. There are rough patches in any marriage. Very early, we understood that there would be times when we disagreed, but there would never be times when we had to be disagreeable."

John and Nellie were married for almost fifty-three years, until Nellie's death in 1985. However, her passing didn't dim John's love for her. On the twenty-first day of every month (she died on March 21), he visited her gravesite and also wrote her a love letter. Coach Wooden kept up this monthly labor of love for almost twenty-five years—the letters piling up in the couple's home—until his deteriorating health and failing eyesight got the best of him. But the love in his heart remained strong, until he died in 2010, just a few months short of his 100th birthday.

The legendary coach would tell anyone who asked, "I had a successful basketball career, but I believe I had an even more successful marriage."

Whatsoever things are true, whatsoever things are honest, whatsoever things are just, whatsoever things are pure, whatsoever things are lovely, whatsoever things are of good report; if there be any virtue, and if there be any praise, think on these things.

PHILIPPIANS 4:8 KJV

*L*ove is more than passion. Passion is temporary. It isn't lasting. Love, real love, lasts.

JOHN WOODEN

True Love Trivia

The day after comedian Jack Benny died,
his wife, Mary, received a single red rose.
The rosy deliveries continued
for the rest of Mary's life—due to a
provision that Jack included in his will.

6

Relax—sometimes the matchmakers are wrong.

Ray and Brianna Morgan
MARRIED MARCH 12, 1957

If Ray Morgan had listened to his family and friends, he would have married Brianna's older sister.

"Everyone was telling me that Bri's sister and I were 'just perfect for each other!'" Ray recalls, with a chuckle. "That sister and I were both gregarious and outrageous. We were both performers. Just give us an audience, and watch out!"

Ray dated Brianna's sister a few times, and they enjoyed each other's company. However, it was younger Brianna—shy, introspective, and performance-phobic—who ended up capturing Ray's heart. Quietly and subtly, but permanently.

"Looking back on things," Ray notes, "Bri's sister and I would have clashed terribly if we had tied the ol' knot. We both need to be in the spotlight all of the time, and we both tend to dominate conversations.

"Bri and I, on the other hand…we complement each other. We balance each other. I've helped her become more comfortable in social situations, and she has taught me the immense value of closing my mouth once in a while—to truly listen to others and contemplate the God-given wonder that is life."

Bri flashes a shy smile at her husband. A smile that speaks volumes.

The lines of purpose in your lives never grow slack, tightly tied as they are to your future in heaven, kept taut by hope. The Message is as true among you today as when you first heard it.

COLOSSIANS 1:5–6 MSG

God can fashion anything out of a simple lump of clay, and He can fashion a strong lasting love out of two very different individuals.

RHONDA S. HOGAN

7

Believe in the firm foundation called Faith.

Larry and Freda Brink

MARRIED JANUARY 23, 1947

In an old two-story house on a quaint lakeside road in Traverse City, Michigan, Larry and Freda Brink stand as proof that a relationship with a strong foundation can endure the passing of years, personal tragedy, and even a world war.

After the couple met and began courting, Larry's family moved from Houston, Texas, to Michigan—separating the two teenage lovers for ten months. Then, just after the duo was reunited, Larry was shipped off to serve in World War II. He would spend the next ten years in the military, where he would serve in the Army Air Force (a precursor to today's Air Force) and the National Guard. Before he left for Germany, England, and other war-time posts, Larry consoled Freda with a few simple words, which proved to be prophetic.

"Larry said to me, 'If this is the real thing, it'll last,'" Freda recalls.

Neither the years nor the distance weakened Larry and Freda's bond of love. Following Larry's safe return from Europe, he and Freda were married in 1947. The couple raised eight biological children and one adopted boy. They also opened their home to a wide and colorful variety of people in need.

Larry credits two factors for keeping the Brink marriage strong for more than sixty-five years. "You have to respect *and* trust the one you choose to spend your life with," he says.

As for his loving wife?

"I just didn't feel right without him," Freda explains. "When you are in love with someone, you feel like you need to be around that person. It helps you to be complete. When each of my nine kids had a serious romance, I asked them to carefully consider the object of their affection. I always said, 'If you can live without 'em, then live without 'em. But if you truly cannot live without this person, then by all means…*don't!*'"

Like most married couples, the Brinks have endured stretches of rough road along their life's journey. They credit being sensitive to each other's feelings, having a sense of humor, and maintaining a strong faith for bringing them to where they are today.

"You have to have the ability to see the other person's side of situations, and be willing to compromise and accept differences," Larry explains.

"And those differences are not necessarily a bad thing. Life gets pretty dull if you never have any heated conversations," Freda adds, with a laugh.

Through challenges large and small, Larry and Freda say that God's divine touch has been ever-present in their lives.

"We were both Christians when we first fell in love," Freda says, "and we strongly felt that it was God's will that we be married, that we be together. I think that was the most important thing—that we both knew we were in God's plan. And it was a very satisfying, happy thing for us because of that security. There wasn't any doubt in either of us."

. . . .

WHEN YOU ARE IN LOVE WITH SOMEONE,
YOU FEEL LIKE YOU NEED TO BE AROUND THAT
PERSON. IT HELPS YOU TO BE COMPLETE.

. . . .

This faith-backed certainty has carried the couple through a lot. The sudden death of one of their sons. Quadruple-bypass surgery for Freda, and Larry's current battle with cancer, to name but a few of the challenges.

"No matter what happens," Freda says confidently, "we know God will be with us today, just as He has been with us every single day of our lives."

*Surely your goodness and love
will follow me all the days of
my life, and I will dwell in the
house of the LORD forever.*

PSALM 23:6

If ever comes a day when we
can't be together, keep me in your
heart, I'll stay there forever.

A.A. MILNE

8

Respect the institution, but <u>love</u> the person.

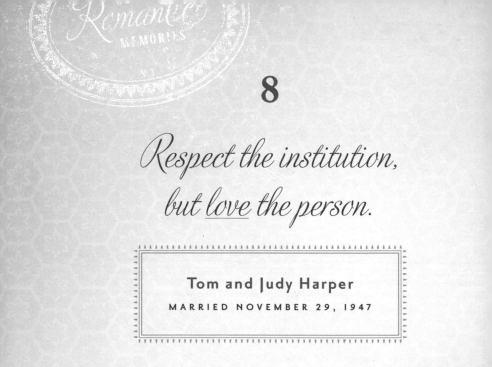

Tom and Judy Harper
MARRIED NOVEMBER 29, 1947

Much is said about the importance of "being committed to marriage." But for the Harpers, commitment to an institution—even one as time-honored as marriage—left them a bit cold.

"I do believe strongly in the institution of marriage," Tom says, "but I've always focused on being committed to Judy, to her as a *person*. A person who happens to be the love of my life. That's what she'll always be."

Judy adds, "Our love and passion are for *each other*. That's what inspires us every day. That is what has brought us through some very difficult times. Illnesses. Crumbling finances. The physical changes that age inevitably brings. What I have learned through it all is this:

You can respect, even *revere*, an institution or an ideal, but I've never been in love with one of those things. I'm in love with Tom Harper. I always will be."

> *Set me as a seal upon your heart,*
> *As a seal upon your arm;*
> *For love is strong as death,*
> *Passion fierce as the grave.*
> *Its flashes are flashes of fire,*
> *A raging flame.*
> *Many waters cannot quench love,*
> *Neither can floods drown it.*
> *If one offered for love*
> *All the wealth of his house,*
> *It would be utterly scorned.*

SONG OF SOLOMON 8:6–7 NRSV

*L*ove at first sight is easy to understand; it's when two people have been looking at each other for a lifetime that it becomes a miracle.

SAM LEVENSON

9

*Keep in mind who
is Number One.
(Hint: It's not you.)*

The book *Wake Up and Smell the Pizza* says it well: "When you keep score in a relationship, everyone loses." The concept of winning and losing might be applicable in the business world, as it is in the athletic arena. But in *marriage*? Think about it: if you "win" at the expense of your husband or wife, have you truly won?

The Achtons, ever since they were married in Grenada, Kansas, some 60 years ago, have sought to work for each other's happiness and fulfillment first.

"You must esteem the other person as more important than yourself," Ken says. "That's what Jesus taught. By the way, I'm not saying this as a secret to getting your own way in the end. This is not a tactic or a strategy. This is about keeping your marriage together!"

Betty agrees.

"In marriage, when you try to get the better of your spouse, you lose—even when you 'win,'" she says. "So many people get hung up on being right, being honored, being vindicated, or being first. My suggestion is to forget all of that stuff. Be full of grace. Be loving. You'll love where that takes you. You might just find yourself celebrating a golden wedding anniversary!"

Love never gives up. Love cares more for others than for self. Love doesn't want what it doesn't have...doesn't force itself on others, isn't always "me first," doesn't fly off the handle, doesn't keep score of the sins of others...puts up with anything, trusts God always, always looks for the best, never looks back, but keeps going to the end.

I CORINTHIANS 13:4–7 MSG

*L*ove is like a tennis match; you'll never win consistently until you learn to serve well.

DAN P. HEROD

10

Understand that tolerance is a decision.

Claude and Mary Stansberry

MARRIED JULY 31, 1946

Claude Stansberry's patience was tested early in his marriage to Mary. Their wedding night was a short one. Claude was roused at 5 a.m. by Mary's dad, who needed help spike-pitching sheaves of oats onto hayricks on the family's Iowa farm. While Claude toiled all day, Mary prepared and served food to neighboring farmers, enduring (with a smile) their wisecracks about newlyweds and abbreviated wedding nights.

Today, Claude and Mary say that the less-than-romantic beginning was good preparation for married life.

"Marriage isn't all fun and games," Claude says. "Some hard work toward getting the job done is necessary. And hard work builds patience and endurance."

Later, the couple settled into their life together, learning to adjust to one another's "quirks and oddities—which are never revealed in the courtship process," as Claude puts it.

He adds, "My mother-in-law ascribed most of the undesirable traits to me, while crediting Mary with the inherent compulsion to correct all of my shortcomings."

The most serious time of adjustment for the Stansberrys came when, in Claude's words, "I was removed from Mary's presence and inflicted on the United States Army."

Upon his return from the service, Claude says he still had the same quirks and oddities—along with a few newly acquired ones, which Mary would need to correct. But once home, he found a very grateful and very tolerant wife.

"I didn't know if she had just decided to put up with me," he recalls, "or if the whole thing was part of a long-term strategy for my improvement, which she had developed while I was away. Eventually, I learned that she had simply *decided* to be tolerant, for which I am extremely thankful. Because, even after years and years of trying, I am not yet perfect in all things. My wife deserves the greatest credit for our long-lasting marriage."

The Stansberrys' advice to other couples is simple—and a product of their gratitude to God for Claude's safe return from military service.

"You need to respect each other's space," Mary says, "and you really do owe your spouse the acceptance of who they are as a person."

Be strong and courageous, and act;
do not fear nor be dismayed, for the
LORD God, my God, is with you. He
will not fail you nor forsake you.

I CHRONICLES 28:20 NASB

To love deeply in one direction
makes us more loving in all others.

ANNE-SOPHIE SWETCHINE

True Love Trivia

At parties, the renowned inventor
Thomas Edison and his wife, Mina, secretly
communicated with each other by tapping
out Morse-code messages into the palms
of one another's hands. Edison even
used this method to propose to Mina.

11

Remember that love has the power to heal.

Ralph and Evelynn Sellers
MARRIED NOVEMBER 22, 1957

Being married for more than 50 years has helped Evelynn and Ralph Sellers truly appreciate the healing power of love.

"In our early days together," Ralph recalls, "Evelynn made my heart hurt—and I mean in a good way. The love between us was so new and so strong. Sometimes it felt like more than my heart could take."

Today, Ralph reveals, life's challenges sometimes make his heart hurt too—but *not* in a good way. "But when that happens," he says, "Evelynn always makes my heart feel better. It's amazing to me. I know some people whose past hurts have kept them from beginning a relationship—or staying in a relationship. I wish I could help them understand that really loving one another might be just the thing they need to start healing those hurts. It's amazing what love can do. God knows that I am living proof."

Bear with each other and forgive one another if any of you has a grievance against someone. Forgive as the Lord forgave you. And over all these virtues put on love, which binds them all together in perfect unity.

COLOSSIANS 3:13–14

When faith is small and hope doubts, love conquers.

THELMA WELLS

12

You'll find "perfection" when you stop looking for it— or demanding it.

Eric and Sara Phillips

MARRIED APRIL 21, 1951

Few burdens are as heavy to carry as the weight of someone else's unrealistic expectations—especially when those expectations come from a person you love deeply. Early in their marriage, Eric and Sara Phillips expected each other to be skilled at various aspects of marriage and running a household. They quickly became frustrated with one another.

"It was only after we acknowledged that we were both 'new at this,'" Sara recalls, "that we quit putting so much pressure on each other. We gave ourselves time to learn and grow. We showed each other grace, the way God wants us to."

Eric adds, "Once that pressure was off, we began to see how hard the two of us were trying. That helped us appreciate each other's *efforts*, even when the actual results weren't perfect. Because, you know, they rarely are. But if your heart is in the right place, you can be *good enough* most of the time."

> *Be patient...attentive to individual needs. And be careful that when you get on each other's nerves you don't snap at each other. Look for the best in each other, and always do your best to bring it out.*
>
> I THESSALONIANS 5:14-15 MSG

The greatest happiness in life is
the conviction that we are loved—
loved for ourselves, or rather,
loved in spite of ourselves.

VICTOR HUGO

13

Understand that marriage doesn't take care of itself.

Carol and Philip Bell
MARRIED JANUARY 10, 1958

Marriage is much like any other significant life endeavor: You get out of it what you put into it. But this truth isn't necessarily self-evident.

After their wedding, the Bells threw themselves into their respective careers—Carol as a teacher and Philip as a pastor. They assumed, in Philip's words, that "the marriage would take care of itself—kind of like auto-pilot, I guess."

Of course, life doesn't work that way. Carol's and Philip's careers flourished, but the teacher and the pastor found themselves losing their tempers, hurting one another's feelings, and having long conversations in which neither spouse truly listened to the other.

"We learned the hard way," Carol admits, "that a marriage that lasts is going to require as much dedication, time, and energy as a career. Make that *more* effort! You have to really listen to your spouse. You have to work at being patient. You have to spend time together. And I am talking about meaningful, fully engaged time. Not just watching TV together. You have to address problems head-on and work together to solve them. You have to live out those vows you made before God."

"Once we started really working at our marriage," Philip says, "it began to thrive. That's why, more than fifty years later, we're still working. I like to say that work *works*."

Love from the center of who you are;
don't fake it. Run for dear life from
evil; hold on for dear life to good.

ROMANS 12:9–10 MSG

*G*od has given us two hands—one to
receive with and the other to give with.
We are not cisterns made for hoarding;
we are channels made for sharing.

BILLY GRAHAM

14

Look for ways to improve

your marriage—

instead of looking for

escape hatches.

Harold and Norma Summers

MARRIED JUNE 20, 1955

In myriad ways, life today is better than it was back in the mid-twentieth century. But not everything has improved, according to Harold and Norma Summers.

The Summerses, whose union took place in Uniontown, Pennsylvania, cast a disappointed eye at today's complicated prenuptial agreements, easy-out divorces, and celebrity serial marriages.

"They didn't give you an escape clause back in our day," Norma says. "We took marriage *seriously* from the get-go, and that's been important to us. We made promises to God and to each other. In front of a church-full of people.

"We believe that if you continually have your eye out for the exit signs, you're not going to be fully engaged—or fully committed—in your marriage. So quit fidgeting. Settle in and attend to the business at hand. You might just have the time of your life."

"I know that I sure have!" Harold adds with a wink. "There's no escaping that fact!"

> *Go after a life of love as if your*
> *life depended on it—because it does.*
> *Give yourself to the gifts God gives you.*

1 CORINTHIANS 14:1 MSG

To love or not; in this
we stand or fall.

JOHN MILTON

15

Give the gifts of love.

Jay and Esther Hafer

MARRIED JANUARY 5, 1936

Every mature couple knows that there's much more to a marriage than the gifts one receives for Valentine's Day, a wedding anniversary, or a birthday.

But there are certain gifts that have a way of capturing what a marriage is all about. Jay and Esther Hafer both came from humble backgrounds. When they began courting, they didn't spend hours on the phone. Neither household had one. Their dates consisted of sitting on an aunt's porch swing and talking for hours.

When the two 19-year-olds married, they couldn't go on a honeymoon, as Jay had no vacation time accrued at work. They married on a Sunday afternoon—Jay in the same suit he wore to his high school graduation and Esther in a white satin dress made by her sister. As neither had a car, they hitched a ride to the church with the best man. Jay woke up at 5:30 a.m. the next day and went to work for a seismographic crew, just like always. He also served in the Colorado National Guard, eventually rising to the rank of sergeant.

Seven years into their marriage, the Hafers still weren't able to afford a house. Their apartment had neither a toilet nor a shower. (These were housed in a separate public building.) Jay continued his work on the seismograph crew, and Esther mended nylon pantyhose for people, for "fifteen cents a run." (Her skills were in high demand, as World War II meant that new nylons were virtually impossible to find.) A big night out consisted of long walks near their apartment. Appropriately, "their song" was "Walking My Baby Back Home."

One day, Jay surprised Esther with a gift. She had never owned a wristwatch, and he presented her with a fashionable Bulova.

"To this day, I don't know how he did that for me," Esther says, shaking her head in wonder. "This was war time, 1943. There were simply no watches available anywhere! It meant so much to me. That's why I still have that watch, more than sixty-five years later. It's the only watch I've ever owned. It's the only one I'll ever need."

Years later, while working as a church secretary, Esther was able to repay her husband's gesture. "In 1970," she says, "Jay was working as a hospital chaplain, making 500 bedside calls every single week. He was striving to minister to patients and their families in some of the most difficult circumstances. He also led three chapel services a week. Two every

Sunday and another on Thursday. So I wanted to do something nice for him. I bought him a ring with a small diamond in it, for one hundred dollars. I know it meant a lot to him. He wore it every day for the rest of his life."

Esther says that these gifts, relatively grand gestures arising out of challenging times, epitomize their marriage.

"It's been meager at times," she says, "but it's also been heaven. Absolute heaven."

Walk in the way of love, just as Christ loved us and gave himself up for us as a fragrant offering and sacrifice to God.

EPHESIANS 5:2

*L*ove grows from our capacity to give what is deepest within ourselves and also receive what is the deepest within another person. The heart becomes an ocean strong and deep, launching all on its tide.

UNKNOWN

True Love Trivia

The wedding band that President
Abraham Lincoln gave Mary Todd Lincoln
was engraved with these words:
"Love is eternal."

16

Don't assume the "I love yous."

Wade and Stephanie Strock
MARRIED AUGUST 9, 1941

After years of marriage, a husband and wife might begin to assume their love for each other is a given. Pleas for a little bit of assurance might be met with comebacks like, "Of course I love you; I'm still married to you, aren't I? Quit being so insecure."

This is a little like assuming that a person can't be sick because there's medicine somewhere in the house. Loving words can be like medicine for the soul. They build a person up when he or she is sagging emotionally, physically, or spiritually. Sharing words or other expressions of love also strengthen two people as a *couple*.

"I can be sinking in a quicksand of despair," Wade Strock explains, "and a few loving words, or a love note or card from Steph can make me feel like I'm walking on air. I feel bullet-proof. I feel young again. It's amazing the power that 'I love you' has."

Stephanie agrees.

"Whether you whisper it, shout it, write it, or even sing it," she says, her voice filling with emotion, "tell your partner, *today*, 'I love you.'"

"I love you too," Wade says. "I always will. And I always will tell you so."

Gracious speech is like clover
honey—good taste to the soul,
quick energy for the body.

PROVERBS 16:24 MSG

I bring you the gift of these four
words: I believe in you.

BLAISE PASCAL

17

Remember: Fifty years happen one day at a time.

Lionel and Carlita Robertson

MARRIED AUGUST 30, 1940

"How do you eat an elephant?" the question goes.

The answer, of course: "One bite at a time."

It's the same with marriage. A marriage, even one as enduring as Lionel and Carlita Robertsons', happens one day at a time. This simple truth has made a profound impact in the couple's life.

Carlita explains, "When we were going through bad times—or having a big hairy fight—I didn't say, 'Oh, no! How am I going to endure fifty years of *this*?' I merely focused on how to get through 'this hour, this day.' Otherwise, the whole thing can seem too overwhelming."

An avid quilter, Carlita has found a metaphor for marriage in her craft.

"I look at marriage the same way I look at a patchwork quilt," she says. "Every stitch is like a minute, every patch like a day. If you just focus on what's in front of you right now, after a while you will have a big beautiful result—when all of those individual things are joined together."

Lionel adds, "Carlita's quilts have kept our bodies warm during our marriage. But she's the one who has always warmed my heart. Day after day and year after year."

This is the day which
the LORD hath made;
we will rejoice and
be glad in it.

PSALM 118:24 KJV

*I*n love, as in other matters,
the young are just beginners.

ISAAC BASHEVIS SINGER

18

Common goals = common bonds.

Ervin and Nichole Standifer

MARRIED JULY 13, 1950

Certainly, a couple doesn't need to do *everything* together, but they shouldn't live lives that are effectively separate either. They need to share more than a bed, a bathroom, and an occasional meal.

Ervin and Nichole Standifer recently retired from their careers (salesman and receptionist, respectively), and they have been volunteering at their local church—serving as greeters and ushers and helping with various refurbishment projects.

"Throughout our marriage, we found lots of projects to collaborate on," Ervin says, "such as home improvement. But on the career front, we worked in different fields, in different types of jobs.

"Now that we are retired, it is great to be volunteers who work *together*. We feel like we're working for the same company, or playing for the same team."

"I highly recommend some kind of joint endeavor for all couples," Nichole says, "whether you're volunteering together or taking karate lessons together. It really builds a sense of camaraderie between the two of you. Working together really works wonders."

If you are really eager to give, then it isn't
important how much you have to give.
God wants you to give what you
have, not what you haven't.

2 CORINTHIANS 8:12 TLB

All that I love loses half its pleasure
if you are not there to share it.

CLARA ORTEGA

19

Flexibility—it's not just for your tendons, ligaments, and muscles.

Georgette and Richard Berry

MARRIED MARCH 11, 1957

Maybe the Rolling Stones were right: "You can't always get what you want." That statement rings true for many aspects of life, including marriage. During their 50-plus years together, the Berrys have faced a mountain of disappointments: lay-offs, a serious illness for Richard, and several seasons of bleak finances. These challenges strained the bonds of their marriage, but Richard and Georgette faced it all with a "bend, but don't break" philosophy.

"It's just a fact," Richard says: "Life is not going to turn out exactly the way you hope. After all, no one *hopes* to become seriously ill, get fired, or have a marriage hit the rocks. But it happens. So, you have to make adjustments. You have to come up with a Plan B—or even a Plan C or D. You have to be willing to regroup and ask for God's help and direction."

Georgette notes, "I wish all young couples would be told that it's not a question of *if* you will face some serious challenge in your life and marriage; it's a question of *when*. Then they'd be better prepared to adapt to change, and to let go of the things that one simply can't control.

"Richard and I might not be as flexible physically as we once were, but mentally, emotionally, and spiritually we're dadgum ballet dancers!"

I've learned by now to be quite content
whatever my circumstances. I'm just as
happy with little as with much....
Whatever I have, wherever I am,
I can make it through anything in
the One who makes me who I am.

PHILIPPIANS 4:10 MSG

The key to a happy marriage is
spending more time counting
blessings than counting troubles.

REV. JERRY SPRINGSTON

20

Major on the majors.

John and Janice Booker

MARRIED JANUARY 19, 1957

The Bookers have a saying that has served them well through decades of marriage: "You'll be just about as miserable as you make up your mind to be."

"These days," Janice says, "I laugh when I think about the stuff that used to set me off: the noisy refrigerator, the cabinet door that didn't shut properly, the route John took when we drove to church, the birds that started chirping too early in the morning. And John had his little pet peeves too. For example, he absolutely hated it when I popped my knuckles. That drove him bonkers."

Several years into their marriage, John and Janice realized that their many small irritations were sapping their time, energy, and focus away from each other's emotional needs, their financial planning, and big-picture life goals. Too many little things were taking up too much room in their lives.

"Learning to let all that little stuff go was a turning point for our marriage," Janice asserts. "One day, we just determined to refuse to let a bunch of petty stuff sabotage us anymore. We put each other on notice. We'd catch each other going off about some dumb thing, and one or the other of us would say, 'Is it worth it? Really? Do we actually want to spend the next five hours kvetching about…whatever?'"

Today, five and a half decades, three children, and two colon cancer surgeries later, the Bookers are grateful they knew what to let go—and when to let go of it.

. . . .

LEARNING TO LET ALL THAT LITTLE STUFF GO
WAS A TURNING POINT FOR OUR MARRIAGE.

. . . .

"It's such a gift," Janice says, "to live a thankful life and realize how blessed by God you are if you have a roof over your head, some food to eat, good people in your life, and your basic health. Even if it took me two surgeries to get where I am now. I don't know how much time John and I have left on this earth, but I do know that we'll spend it focusing on what's truly important. All couples would do well to do the same."

The Lord is near. Do not be anxious about anything, but in every situation, by prayer and petition, with thanksgiving, present your requests to God. And the peace of God, which transcends all understanding, will guard your hearts and your minds in Christ Jesus.

PHILIPPIANS 4:5–7

Sooner or later we begin to understand that love is more than verses on valentines and romance in the movies. We begin to know that love is here and now, real and true, the most important thing in our lives, the greatest treasure of all.

UNKNOWN

True Love Trivia

The honor for the living couple with the longest
marriage goes to Bradford, England's Karan
and Kartari Chand. As this book goes to press,
the Chands have been married for 87 and a half
years. "We know that being married for 87 years
is a blessing," Kartari told the *Yorkshire Post*
in early 2012, "but equally we will be ready
to go when it's time. It's all up to the will of
God, but we really have lived a good life."

21

Never underestimate the value of patience and empathy.

Zach and Rhonda Hollister

MARRIED JANUARY 9, 1958

Zach Hollister is a character. He strikes up lively conversations with complete strangers. He will burst into song—without warning or sense of melody—even in a busy restaurant or packed elevator. A simple trip to the grocery store can suddenly turn into a surprise weekend getaway.

Fortunately, Zach *knows* he's a live wire. One key to a successful marriage, according to him, is being acutely aware of one's quirks. It's equally important to truly appreciate the spouse who puts up with said quirks.

Indeed, there's a special place in heaven for the husband of the woman driven to pursue a career on the Broadway stage. The wife of the man who insists on racing dirt bikes well into his fifties. The spouse of the freelance artist whose income (and mood swings) are as unpredictable as the weather.

A character like Zach can bring a lot to a relationship—excitement, adventure, energy, and passion—but all of that zing comes with a hefty price tag. Finding the person who's willing to pay is a key.

"I knew Rhonda was the right one for me," Zach says. "I knew she'd be up for the adventure that our life has been. Conversely, I also knew that none of the other women I'd dated would be able to put up with me."

Rhonda has been putting up with Zach for more than 50 years now—since their wedding in Wheeling, West Virginia. She says she wouldn't have it any other way.

"Yes, he's a handful sometimes; he's a character," she admits with a smile. "But he's a character with a lot of *character*. And that makes all the difference in the world."

Accept one another then, just as Christ accepted
you, in order to bring praise to God.

ROMANS 15:7

*L*ove isn't like a reservoir. You'll never drain it dry. It's much more like a natural spring. The longer and farther it flows, the stronger and deeper it becomes.

EDDIE CANTOR

22

Golden Rule =
a golden anniversary.

Rick and Jean Martin
MARRIED MARCH 12, 1957

"I was raised on the Golden Rule," Rick Martin says, "and I've done a pretty good job of living by it. With one notable exception: My poor, longsuffering wife. With everyone else, I was treating them the way I'd like to be treated, but when it came to Jean, I was treating her whatever old way my mood dictated. And often I was cranky and tired—probably from being so darned nice to everyone else."

Rick says he experienced an epiphany one day when a coworker at his office was rude to him. Rick stomped away from the encounter, fuming silently, *How would you like it if I treated YOU that way?!*

"I'm not sure how that incident at the office led my thoughts toward Jean," Rick says, "but it did. I guess God does work in mysterious ways. Anyway, the whole thing brought me to my knees with guilt."

Before he went home that night, Rick made a list detailing how he'd like to be treated. The list included words like respect, kindness, patience, thoughtfulness, gratefulness, forgiveness, and love. From that moment on, he made a practice of reviewing the list every night before returning home to Jean.

She noticed the change right away.

"I remember that she asked me, 'Why are you being so nice to me?'" Rick recalls. "That cut me to the quick. I realized how much I needed to change."

But Rick did change, as evidenced by the message Jean wrote in her fiftieth anniversary card to him. She closed with, "Thank you so much for treating me like your princess. That means the world to me!"

Treat others the same way you
want them to treat you.

LUKE 6:31 NASB

*L*ove is, above all, the gift of oneself.

JEAN ANOUILH

23

Ask, "Who can I be imperfect with?"

Joy and Alex Dominguez
MARRIED JULY 14, 1953

We all know the painstaking preparation one goes through for a date—especially a Big Date, on Valentine's Day, New Year's Eve, or a birthday. Male or female, we want to look our best, smell our best, and act our best. So every stray hair is plucked or trimmed. Every flaw is eliminated—or at least cleverly disguised. Conversations are rehearsed. Directions to that new restaurant or movie theater are checked and re-checked.

But no one can look perfect, smell perfect, or act perfect all the time. Especially in a long-term relationship in which two people share the same living space—including the same bedroom and bathroom. So, what happens when the defenses are down, the makeup is off, the hair is messed up, the breath reeks, and the stomach simply cannot be sucked in any longer?

For Joy Dominguez, these questions separated Alex from all the other potential mates.

"When I really thought about a life with someone," she explains, "it became very clear to me that I didn't want anyone but Alex watching me drool while I slept. Even with such a vulnerable, potentially embarrassing situation like that in my mind's eye, I felt okay about it—felt safe about it—when I thought of Alex. I honestly couldn't say I felt that way about anybody else."

Alex found the same kind of acceptance and security in Joy, and that's why, almost 60 years later, they are still loving each other—drool, morning breath, bed-head, fumbled words, and all.

You're blessed when you're content with just who you are—no more, no less. That's the moment you find yourselves proud owners of everything that can't be bought.

MATTHEW 5:5 MSG

You come to love not by finding the perfect person, but by seeing an imperfect person perfectly.

SAM KEEN

24

Enjoy the sounds of silence.

Shelly and Jedd Thomason

MARRIED JUNE 6, 1953

Shelly and Jedd Thomason don't discount all of the focus on a couple's need to communicate with one another. Good communication has been a cornerstone of their long union. But Jedd realized that he and Shelly were perfect for each other one day when the talking stopped.

"You hear a lot about 'uncomfortable silences,'" Jedd explains, "and I had my share of those while out on a date. You feel like you have to keep talking or have music playing or have some form of entertainment or distraction going on. That's because two people can feel awkward when things go silent.

"But it was different with me and Shelly—right from the start. We could have a great conversation or enjoy a TV show together. But then, when the talking stopped or we turned off the TV, we found that we could sit peacefully and quietly, simply enjoying one another's company. To this day, she is the only one I can sit with when the TV is off. Or ride in the car with—with the radio off and nothing in the CD player. I tend to get antsy around other people. Even some of my close friends. But never, ever with Shelly."

"I believe that those quiet moments are a true test of a relationship, any relationship," Shelly adds. "You know you are with a soul mate when neither of you feels pressured to keep the noise going. All of that stuff can be a distraction from the tension or uneasiness that can lurk in some relationships. But I am at perfect peace, just sitting in a quiet room with my husband, enjoying a comfortable silence. To me, it feels like home."

If I speak with human eloquence and
angelic ecstasy but don't love, I'm nothing
but the creaking of a rusty gate.

I CORINTHIANS 13:1 MSG

*A*t one glance, I love you with
a thousand hearts.

MIHRI HATUN

25

A house is made of many bricks.

Jeff and Tolanda Jackson
MARRIED JULY 21, 1956

Great causes have brought many a couple together. A shared passion for teaching, serving the needy, or campaigning for a political candidate can create a romantic spark.

For the Jacksons, who were married in Whitefish, Montana, the catalyst was something more mundane: green bean casserole.

"What first drew me to Jeff?" Tolanda recalls, "We both love green bean casserole."

It's not the stuff of Shakespeare or the silver screen. But once Jeff and Tolanda found common ground in the all-important side-dish category, they moved on to other areas in which they shared interests and passion, such as a healthy work ethic, an enduring belief in love, and a strong faith.

Marriages like the Jacksons are a great reminder that those shared quirks can sometimes mean a lot—and that it's worth one's noting who's eyeing the same items at the buffet restaurant or church potluck dinner.

Live joyfully with the wife whom thou lovest.

ECCLESIASTES 9:9 KJV

A happy life is simply the sum of many small, happy moments.

PENNY KRUGMAN

True Love Trivia

Wedding cake was originally designed to be thrown at the bride and groom, just as we toss rice or birdseed today. Fortunately, the projectile brand of wedding cake was not frosted, making the custom less messy for both the hurlers and their targets.

26

Don't forget your <u>meditation</u>.

Dom and Winnie Jansen
MARRIED MARCH 27, 1946

Have you ever been caught up in a marital argument that feels like sprinting around and around the same track—in Hades?

Even mature couples can get caught in the cruel race, visiting the same problems again and again. The only thing that changes is the level of frustration and anger. And the change is not for the better.

"Winnie and I are 'good' arguers," Dom explains, "but sometimes life's problems stretch you beyond your abilities and beyond your patience. Sometimes she and I would get in an argument, and two hours later we hadn't solved anything. We were just spinning our wheels. Which put us in a deep rut."

During the middle of one such conflict, Winnie suggested something she had heard from a friend: "I know this sounds unromantic, but sometimes a husband and wife simply need to get out of each other's face for a while. Sometimes you gotta give each other some space."

Thus, Winnie and Dom retreated to neutral parts of their house to be quiet with their thoughts. For Winnie, this meant praying. For Dom, it meant meditating and reciting Scriptures to calm his nerves, settle his mind, and quiet his heart—both literally and figuratively.

"We've found that some time of peaceful soul-seeking, reflection, and contemplation can work wonders," Winnie says. "Sometimes it provides the answers you need, right then and there. But even when it doesn't, it puts you in a better state of mind and spirit to find those answers, eventually. And we've always been able to find them—thank the good Lord!"

Don't use your anger as fuel for revenge. And don't stay angry. Don't go to bed angry. Don't give the Devil that kind of foothold in your life.

EPHESIANS 4:26 MSG

What counts in making a happy marriage is not so much how compatible you are, but how you deal with incompatibility.

LEO TOLSTOY

27

Learn from others' mistakes.

Thomas and Mary Johnson

MARRIED JUNE 14, 1958

"Don't get me wrong," Thomas Johnson says, "I don't enjoy watching people around me getting divorces, especially when it happens to family members or close friends. But at the same time, you'd be a fool not to notice the mistakes people make and try to avoid them in your own marriage. You need to learn from life."

During their 50-plus years of marriage, the Johnsons say they have seen three primary mistakes that damage or end marriages.

Dishonesty. "You have to be able to trust each other," Mary says, "and you can't trust someone who's dishonest. So tell the truth, even about the little things. Make honesty a habit."

Unresolved conflict or bitterness. "You can't let things fester," Thomas asserts. "That kind of approach will eat away at you, and it will affect how you treat your spouse. You'll be angry, impatient, cold, or whatever—without even intending to."

Infidelity. "We've lost track," Mary says, "of how many marriages we've seen end because a man or woman had a fling out of anger, revenge, boredom, or curiosity. You can save yourself years and years of agony, guilt, bitterness, and more—just by staying true."

All you who fear GOD, how blessed you are!
How happily you walk on his smooth straight road!
You worked hard and deserve
all you've got coming.
Enjoy the blessing! Revel in the goodness!

PSALM 128:1-2 MSG

*L*ove is not leisure; it is work.

ANNA QUINDLEN

28

*Make your marriage
better tomorrow
than it is today.*

Patricia and Allen Johnston

MARRIED APRIL 9, 1950

The Johnstons claim that athletics have given their marriage a sporting chance. Patricia and Allen were collegiate athletes who have continued to compete in age-group tennis and running events, respectively. They note that their mindset toward athletic endeavors has made for a winning romance.

Over the years, the couple noted how many of their peers strived to improve in their sports, their hobbies, and their careers. However, when it came to marriage, maintaining the status quo seemed to be the standard goal.

"The only time we saw a couple really working hard on their marriage was when that marriage was in trouble," Patricia notes. "To us, that would be like training for a sport only when you were injured or out of shape. Sports don't work that way, and neither does life."

So, the Johnstons determined that they would pour effort into their marriage every day, so that it would always be getting stronger. It's worked. Today, they both say they are more in love than on the day they were married, and that their marriage is the strongest it's ever been.

"It might be okay to *maintain* your car or maintain your lawn," Allen observes, "but maintain a marriage? No way. You have to work *hard* at it. You must keep making it better. The effort has to be constant. But believe me; you'll be glad you did."

"Oh," Patricia says with a wink, "I believe you, *sport*."

Don't copy the behavior and customs of this world, but let God transform you into a new person by changing the way you think. Then you will learn to know God's will for you, which is good and pleasing and perfect.

ROMANS 12:2 NLT

The art of love…is largely the art of persistence.

ALBERT ELLIS

29

Let the good times "role."

Gene and Carrie Daugherty
MARRIED AUGUST 27, 1939

Sharing is an important part of any strong marriage, but the Daughertys maintain that sharing can be taken too far.

Carrie explains, "You can't share everything all the time. A husband and a wife must have some clear-cut roles. When we first got married, we'd both say things like, 'We need to open a savings account,' or 'We need to make an appointment to have a will drawn up,' or 'We need to find a second car.'

"Well, guess what? 'We' never got around to doing anything!'"

Eventually, Carrie and Gene learned the need to define and delegate duties. Carrie managed the finances and paid the bills. Gene made the medical appointments and picked up prescriptions and other medications. Carrie sorted the mail. Gene made sure the cars were properly maintained and tuned up.

"Having clear roles helps us both play to our strengths," Gene explains. "And it avoids all that useless bickering over whose turn it is to do what. Of course, there are *some* things that are the most fun when done together."

"Gene!" Carrie says. "Shame on you."

Gene smiles innocently.

"I was just talking about *dancing*," he says.

> *It's better to have a partner*
> *than to go it alone. Share the*
> *work, share the wealth. And*
> *if one falls, the other helps.*
>
> ECCLESIASTES 4:9 MSG

*L*ove makes burdens lighter, because
you divide them. It makes joys more
intense, because you share them. It
makes you stronger, so that you can
reach out and become involved with
life in ways you dared not risk alone.

UNKNOWN

30

Appearances are deceiving—but not to those truly in love.

Jim and Neva Springston
MARRIED JUNE 10, 1936

What do you get when you combine a prim and proper school-teacher with an irreverent, Navy-vet auto mechanic who didn't graduate from high school? A marriage that endured for almost fifty-seven years.

Jim and Neva Springston seemed like the classic odd couple. Neva always dressed impeccably and couldn't even bring herself to order "chicken breast" in a restaurant. Jim would jokingly ask dinner guests to refer to Amsterdam as "Amsterdarn," in deference to his wife.

Jim practically lived in his ragged mechanic's coveralls and sported permanent grease under his fingernails. He was fond of sharing a saucy Navy song, story, or saying—even around the grandchildren...or the ladies prayer group. For him, what happened on the aircraft carrier USS *Saratoga* didn't necessarily *stay* on the USS *Saratoga*.

But, despite all of the surface differences—differences that had casual onlookers shaking their heads—the Springstons shared deeper bonds. Their work ethic was virtually unmatched, even when they entered their eighties. They shared a deep faith in God and a steadfast commitment to their family. They thought nothing of driving sixteen hours round-trip to see one of their grandchildren compete in a wrestling match or basketball game or sing in a school musical. And both of them would donate time or money to those in need. Jim fixed many a neighbor's car or truck—often for no more than a "God bless you" as payment.

> DESPITE ALL OF THE SURFACE DIFFERENCES, THEY SHARED A DEEP FAITH IN GOD AND A STEADFAST COMMITMENT TO THEIR FAMILY.

As a young couple, they would often visit their favorite coffee shop. Jim would order a cup of joe, Neva a glass of water. Their bill: five cents. Jim left a quarter tip every time.

Jim and Neva also shared a love for travel, setting a goal to visit all fifty states together. They made it to every one but Hawaii, before Jim's long battle with cancer intervened.

"Visiting all fifty states would have been nice," Neva says, "but that's not the most important thing. What means the most to me is the way we saw all those places—*together*."

The one who blesses others is abundantly blessed; those who help others are helped.

PROVERBS 11:25 MSG

*I*t is only with the heart that one can see rightly, for the most essential things are invisible to the eye.

ANTOINE DE SAINT-EXUPÉRY

True Love Trivia

Many creatures mate for life, including wolves, barn owls, and bald eagles. But the anglerfish takes things to extremes. The tiny male fish finds his beloved by scent, and then holds onto her with his teeth. Soon, the two fish fuse together—literally—bringing new meaning to the phrase "and the two shall become one."

31

Compromise— it's not a dirty word.

Paul and Gunnie Sparrman
MARRIED SEPTEMBER 7, 1957

Philippians 2:4 says, "Each of you should look not only to your own interests, but also to the interests of others." For Paul and Gunnie Sparrman, marriage is the ideal place to put these New Testament words into action.

"After all," Gunnie says, "marriage is the most intense 24/7 relationship God ever invented. A husband and wife must look out for each other and be considerate of one another."

She adds, "Sure, we all have our own interests and needs that we wish to have fulfilled—in the ways that satisfy us best. It's only natural. But when two people get married, they must learn to compromise; to set aside their own agenda for the good of their spouse."

For the past 55 years, Gunnie and Paul have been putting each other first. To their family and friends, this approach appears to be second-nature. Even during a disagreement.

"When we disagree about something," Paul explains, "we take turns letting each other share our thoughts—without interruptions. For us, listening is very, very important."

Mutual respect and affirmation are vital too. If you could eavesdrop on a Sparrman argument, you'd often hear these words from both spouses, even in the heat of battle: "I don't agree with you, but I love you."

Disagreements and difficulties are the times when a husband or wife learns that a spouse's love is for *real*. It's easy to be loving in times of harmony and shared understanding. But true, self-giving love proves its genuine nature when one person gives ground for the sake of another. "It's compromise that works," says Paul, a retired minister. "With the large matters and the small ones."

Gunnie smiles and adds, "That is so true. When we downsized to a retirement apartment, we didn't agree on where to put our television: in the living room or in the den. We went with Paul's choice, and now I see that this was the best place after all. He was right that time. I've been right other times. With us, it's give and take. It always has been."

Gunnie and Paul both humbly claim, "I married up the food chain."

Sports fans call it "out-kicking your coverage." By any name, holding one's spouse in high esteem leads to a respect for his or her opinion, and it builds a foundation of love that can last a lifetime.

The Sparrmans simply refuse to waste time and energy trying to win an argument. Instead, they have developed the uncanny ability to encourage, bless, and spread joy to each other—even during tense times. And this selfless attitude has spilled over to other areas of their life. Whether they are on an airplane, in a doctor's waiting room, or running errands, they look beyond themselves to the needs of others. They are the kind of people who let strangers ahead of them in grocery store lines, who hold doors open, or give up the prime parking space.

"I believe that Paul and Gunnie treat everyone kindly," their daughter-in-law Bonnie Sparrman observes, "because they treat *one another* so kindly."

Agree with each other, love each other, be deep-spirited friends. Don't push your way to the front; don't sweet-talk your way to the top. Put yourself aside, and help others get ahead. Don't be obsessed with getting your own advantage. Forget yourselves long enough to lend a helping hand.

PHILIPPIANS 2:4 MSG

*I*n marriage, sometimes we submit; sometimes we outwit.

RUTH BELL GRAHAM

True Love Trivia

Frances Cleveland was the first bride of a
US president to be married in the White House.
Additionally, the 21-year-old's marriage to
Grover Cleveland made her the youngest-
ever First Lady. Seven years later, Frances gave
birth to Esther Cleveland, the only child ever
born to a First Lady in the White House.

32

Forgive and, yes, forget.

Oliver and Hannah Smith

MARRIED JUNE 21, 1954

"I'm not gonna lie to ya," Oliver Smith says, "I used to hold grudges, big-time. The wife and I both did."

Hannah agrees, casting her eyes downward, "We both struggled to get past that feeling of being wronged. That feeling of being wounded. I would be bitter. Oliver would be distant and aloof—even after the requisite apologies and statements of forgiveness."

Then the Smiths had a revelation, appropriately, in church. Their pastor quoted from Saint Paul's first letter to the Corinthians, noting, "Love keeps no record of wrongs."

"That hit me like a punch to the gut," Oliver recalls. "Because I was an expert bookkeeper when it came to all of the things Hannah did to hurt my feelings or get my goat. So, that sermon was the turning point.

You know, sometimes that verse is a pain in the neck to me, because there are still times when I'd like to have something to hold over her head, some kind of trump card to play when I really need it. But that's not love."

Hannah says, "We've pretty much gotten past the silly holding of grudges. Because when you hold onto a grudge, you can't hold much else. And, even after all these years, I'd rather hold Oliver any day."

Oliver grins.

"How about *today*?" he asks.

> *Smart people know how to hold*
> *their tongue; their grandeur*
> *is to forgive and forget.*
>
> PROVERBS 19:11 MSG

Tis the most tender part of love,
each other to forgive.

JOHN SHEFFIELD

33

Have a few simple rules.

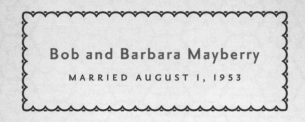

Bob and Barbara Mayberry
MARRIED AUGUST 1, 1953

Relationships can be complicated, but the Mayberrys have seen their marriage not just survive, but thrive, during the past six decades.

Their secret? A few simple rules, free of psychobabble and equivocation.

THE MAYBERRYS' MARRIAGE RULES

Trust each other—and be trustworthy.
Respect one another—in word and in deed.
Be honest.
Keep no secrets from each other.
Strive for real love—beyond physical attraction and sex.

Don't sweat the small stuff. Save your strength for the big stuff.

Don't spend more than you can afford.

"There is nothing glamorous or revolutionary about the rules we've chosen to live by," Bob concedes. "I don't see the title of the next marriage best seller in there anywhere. But this is what has worked for us. After many, many years, we honestly love each other. And we care more deeply for each other right now than we ever have."

Barbara squeezes her husband's hand.

"And that is saying something," she says. "I guess love *rules*."

Use every chance you
have for doing good.

EPHESIANS 5:16 NCV

*L*ove is like a mountain, hard
to climb, but once you get to the
top, the view is beautiful.

DANIEL MONROE TUTTLE

34

*Keep your promises —
there's power in a
promise kept.*

Arthur and Galen Miles
MARRIED SEPTEMBER 8, 1957

Love works in mysterious ways. The Miles's marriage, which began in Akron, Ohio, is one example.

"My first serious boyfriend had dumped me," Galen remembers, "and I was heartbroken. I didn't know how I could ever trust a man again."

Eventually, Galen felt she was ready to give love another try, but she was wary. She shared her fears with Boyfriend Number Two, one Arthur Miles. Rather than be offended or put off by what he heard, Arthur made Galen a simple promise.

"He promised me that he would never dump me," Galen smiles. "And he's been fulfilling that promise for some fifty-five years now. The power of those words erased the pain of the past and gave me sure hope for the future."

"I was very young when I made that promise," Arthur says, "but I was old enough to know about keeping your word. To me, my wedding vows were an extension of that earlier promise—a promise that I'm always going to keep."

"And that," Galen says, "is why my Boyfriend Number Two is really Number One!"

The ways of right-living people
glow with light; the longer they
live, the brighter they shine.

PROVERBS 4:18 MSG

To love abundantly is to
live abundantly, and to love
forever is to live forever.

HENRY DRUMMOND

35

*Manage conflict;
don't let it manage you.*

Georgia and Andrew Brennan
MARRIED JUNE 8, 1957

As a child, Georgia saw her parents fight all the time—right up until their acrimonious divorce.

Conversely, Andrew's parents rarely had a visible conflict. Despite these different upbringings, Georgia and Andrew entered their marriage with the same perception: Conflict was something to be avoided. Conflict was a sign that something was wrong with a marriage.

So when they found themselves stepping on one other's nerves or injuring one another's feelings, Georgia and Andrew retreated to neutral corners—or squeezed pseudo-pleasant words through forced smiles and clenched teeth.

"Conflict was like the cockroaches in our first apartment," Andrew explains. "At first, we thought if we ignored the problem, it would just go away. Of course, that doesn't work. With love or with pest control. Conflict and cockroaches are both hardy critters. And they breed like nobody's business."

Frustrated, Georgia visited her pastor for advice. She was sure there was something wrong with her, her husband, or their marriage. Maybe all three.

"I cannot tell you how *relieved* I was," she recalls, "to hear that what we were going through was common to many marriages. But I also can't tell you how surprised I was to hear the minister say that Andrew and I *needed* to argue. We needed to get that conflict out on the table and deal with it."

The pastor helped Georgia (and, eventually, Andrew) see that conflict is something that needs to be resolved, not ignored.

"I was clamming up and withdrawing when I was unhappy," she recalls. "I found that these were the very times I needed to talk with Andrew, to share my feelings, ask his advice, and express my concerns about something he was doing—or *not* doing. And when we started talking, I learned about some of his disappointment with himself as a new husband. I discovered that all he really needed from me was a little encouragement and support. "

Andrew nods his head in agreement at his wife's words.

"It's funny," he says, "sometimes we'll see a young couple walking hand in hand or sharing a kiss, and my first thought is, *Wow, those two must really be in love.* But I'd get a lot more accurate picture if I saw how they handled an argument. Any two people can hold hands or gaze into each other's eyes. But can you argue constructively and respectfully? Can you actually deal with conflict, rather than tiptoe around it, like it's a sleeping watchdog? That's how you know you have a love that will stand the test of time."

"A love like ours," Georgia adds.

"No argument with that," Andrew says. "No argument whatsoever."

*Most importantly, love each other
deeply, because love will cause people
to forgive each other for many sins.*

I PETER 4:8 NCV

*I*n family life, love is the oil
that eases friction, the cement
that binds closer together, and the
music that brings harmony.

EVA BURROWS

True Love Trivia

During a kiss, nerves carry sensation
from the lips to the brain. The brain
responds by releasing a "love potion" of
sorts: oxytocin, which creates feelings
of affection and attachment; dopamine,
which produces feelings of pleasure;
serotonin, which elevates the mood; and
adrenaline, which increases the heart rate.

36

Share a spiritual journey.

Dave and Dee Clark

MARRIED AUGUST 22, 1954

In 50-plus years of marriage, the Clarks have traveled all over the world together. But they say that the most satisfying journey of their long union has been a journey of faith.

"We had been married about fourteen years before matters of faith or religion were very important to us," Dee recalls. "But as we matured as people, experienced more of life, and did more reading and thinking, we both become convinced that there was more to life than just the physical realm. We both made a commitment to God—first me and then Dave—around the time of our fifteenth anniversary."

"I know that religion can cause tension in marriages," Dave says, "but for us, it actually brought us closer together. Praying together—that is a very intimate and very sacred thing for two people to share."

The Clarks pray together daily and also read many of the same books about spirituality, biblical history, and how faith intersects with contemporary issues. They spend hours every week discussing their journeys of faith—as individuals and as a couple.

"We don't agree on everything," Dee says, "so we are challenged—in a good way—by our differing perspectives. We've had some intriguing, mind-stretching conversations. For example, not long ago during a presidential election we supported different candidates, but we respected how each other's candidate tried to balance his faith with his politics."

"Dee and I have a spiritual intimacy," Dave concludes, "that in some ways is even deeper than our physical or intellectual intimacy. We only wish we'd discovered it sooner. Good thing we're both still, uh, *young*?"

May your unfailing love be with us,
LORD, even as we put our hope in you.

PSALM 33:22

*T*he sweetest reward of your marriage
is not what you get out of it, but
what you become because of it.

REV. ROBERT ST. JOHN

37

Love—with no fine print.

Milt and Darlene S.*

MARRIED JANUARY 19, 1957

Any couple that has been married a few years knows that it's not a question of *if* a marriage will face strife and storms; it's a question of when. Jobs are lost. Health goes south. Investments go sour. Dear friends move away. Children rebel.

Husbands and wives, being human, often respond badly to the challenges life hurls at them. They go through periods of anger, depression, confusion, and unpredictability. Milt and Darlene have seen each other endure all of the above, and more.

It's common for a wife or husband to want out when the other partner is behaving poorly.

"I never knew he had such a temper; it's scary," a wife might say.

"She's put on so much weight," a husband might mutter to himself. "I hate to admit it, but I'm not attracted to her anymore."

Milt and Darlene have seen scenarios like the aforementioned end marriages. But theirs has endured. The secret?

"Not just love," Darlene says emphatically, "but *unconditional* love. Milt and I didn't take it lightly when the preacher said, 'For better or for *worse.*' We had talked about those words before the wedding, and the good Lord knows we've talked 'em to death in the years since! There's a world of meaning in a word like 'worse.'"

Milt and Darlene are quick to note that unconditional love does not mean ignoring a spouse's destructive behavior or attitudes, but it does mean helping each other grow and improve as people, rather than bailing out when a marriage stops being a fairy tale.

"If you truly love and understand someone, you stand by him or her when the heat gets turned up," Milt says. "I'm thankful for Darlene's understanding and forgiveness, especially during those early, rocky times."

"And I'm thankful that you traveled an awful lot back then," Darlene adds, with a wink.

Love covers over all wrongs.

PROVERBS 10:12

To see a young couple loving each other is no wonder, but to see an old couple loving each other is the best sight of all.

WILLIAM MAKEPEACE THACKERAY

*See Editor's Note on page 145.

38

Go the extra mile for peace.

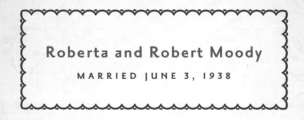

Roberta and Robert Moody

MARRIED JUNE 3, 1938

The Moodys' early months of marriage were marked by the typical feelings of euphoria.

"We were ga-ga over each other," Roberta says. "But after all that ga-ga stuff wore off, we realized just how much we truly *enjoyed* each other's company. We became the best of friends. I put up with Robert's snoring, and he put up with—well, whatever I might do to try to annoy him. I had a whole bag of tricks—believe me."

But even the best of friends quarrel. And what separates the lasting friendships from those more fleeting is how the combatants make *peace*. Roberta recalls one night when she was "madder than a hornet" at her spouse.

Instead of sulking or returning anger for anger, Robert chose another path. In the middle of the night, he rose and crept outside the family house in Vacaville, California. Roberta had no idea what her spouse was up to, and this nocturnal excursion only heightened her anger. Was he leaving her? Was he outside venting his anger on the mailbox?

Her anger subsided in the morning—when she saw the large bouquet of wildflowers her husband had collected for her.

"He picked all kinds of flowers for me," Roberta marvels. "In the pitch-dark. By morning, those flowers were starting to get pretty sorry-looking, but I was touched. And, of course, I forgave him for whatever it was that made me angry. To tell you the truth, I don't even remember what set me off. But I remember what Robert did. He was a true peacemaker that night. And that was not the only time he went the extra mile for peace.

"My dear husband is deceased now, but I hope the example he set will be helpful to other couples. Robert Moody sure set a fine example for me. I hope I followed his lead during our marriage. God knows that I sure did try."

God blesses those who work for peace, for they will be called the children of God.

MATTHEW 5:9 NLT

The quarrels of lovers are the renewal of love.

HORACE

39

Seek help from a Higher Power.

Mr. and Mrs. Bob McDaniel*

MARRIED JUNE 12, 1947

"I know some people might scoff at what I'm about to say," Bob McDaniel states, "but our marriage would have never endured without help from a Higher Power—and I don't mean my mother-in-law!"

After getting married and establishing their first home, the McDaniels found that living in close quarters with a new companion can test one's patience beyond its capacity. Every bad habit and every personal oddity is magnified.

"Things got desperate pretty quickly," Bob recalls, "and we did the only thing we could think of: We prayed. We asked God for strength and patience and wisdom. And we believed—even though it was hard to believe—that He would rescue us."

Bob says those prayers were answered.

"I don't know exactly how it happened," he says, "but somehow, day by day, we received the strength we needed to get by. Our faith in God was rewarded. Some people might chalk it up to our growing maturity or something like that, but we know there is no earthly explanation. And believe me, there's no way on earth my wife would put up with a guy like me for so long without divine intervention!"

> *It's in Christ that we find out who we are and what we're living for. Long before we first heard of Christ and got our hopes up, he had his eye on us, had designs on us for glorious living, part of the overall purpose he is working out in everything and everyone.*
>
> EPHESIANS 1:11 MSG

*T*wo human loves make one divine.

ELIZABETH BARRETT BROWNING

*See Editor's Note on page 145.

40

Get by with a little help from your friends— and family.

"My suitcases were laid out on the bed," Liz Eaton remembers. "I was ready to pack up and leave my husband. Maybe for good."

Liz and her newlywed husband, Rich, had just endured their first major blowup, and Rich had left for work—with a flurry of harsh words, a slam of the front door, and the screech of tires on the driveway. Liz pulled her suitcases out of the closet and then called her best friend, Ann, to help her pack and give her a ride to the airport. Ann arrived promptly, but instead of helping Liz sort and pack her "get-away clothes," she invited her friend to sit by her on the bed and pour out her heart.

"Ann listened attentively to me," Liz says, "not interrupting or judging, but not joining in on my anger at Rich either. When I was done venting, she put her arm around me and asked me, quietly, if I *really* wanted to leave. She asked me if I still loved my husband. She asked me if I still believed in marriage. Those questions really brought me up short. Without lecturing me or preaching a sermon, she helped me see that what I *really* wanted to do was make peace with Rich."

Then Ann made a suggestion. She encouraged Liz to invite her older sister, a high school guidance counselor, to moderate a discussion between the newlyweds.

"Rich resisted that idea at first," Liz recalls. "He was afraid my sister and I were going to gang up on him. But, on the other hand, he's always respected her a lot, so he eventually agreed."

That evening, Liz's sister guided the couple as they sorted through their hurt, frustration, and anger. She helped each of them see where they were at fault. More importantly, she helped them realize anew how much they truly meant to each other.

"We laugh about it now," Liz says. "About how I thought I was calling a get-away accomplice, but what I actually got was the voice of reason. And I can't count how many times my sister or one of my girlfriends has been there for me—or for us—when help was desperately needed.

"Those people were truly God-sends. I think all couples need to realize that they are not alone. Whatever the challenge, it's so nice to be able to call in reinforcements. After all, that's what friends, and family, are for."

Where there is no guidance the people fall, But in abundance of counselors there is victory.

PROVERBS 11:14 NASB

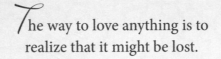

The way to love anything is to realize that it might be lost.

G.K. CHESTERTON

True Love Trivia

Hundreds of years ago in England,
couples who were willing to swear on
the King James Bible that they hadn't
engaged in a marital spat in an entire year
were rewarded with a side of bacon.

41

A heartfelt (but humble) effort works wonders.

Joseph and Ginnie Hathaway
MARRIED JULY 13, 1950

Some couples enter marriage with hearts full of confidence and heads full of advice from marriage experts, and there's certainly nothing wrong with that. To succeed in any endeavor, one needs confidence and knowledge.

But the Hathaways' road to a successful marriage has been paved with different stuff.

"This might sound weird," Joseph says, "but we entered marriage with a lot of humility rather than a sense of boldness, and I think that's been one of the keys to our success. Ginnie and I didn't assume we'd be great at marriage. Not even 'very good' at it.

"We didn't stand in the front of a church on our wedding day with this smug feeling that we were about to embark on the best marriage of all time—the kind that people make movies about."

Ginnie agrees: "We just said, 'Hey, we really love each other; let's try to pull this off, for as long as we can.'"

As the years rolled by, the Hathaways' humility served them well. It made them eager to learn from other couples, as well as from various books and conferences about relationships. And it kept them from assuming that a happy marriage was an entitlement.

"We understood, from day one, that this relationship was something we'd have to keep working at," Ginnie says. "It wasn't going to happen by itself, just because Joe and I are such swell people. We prayed for our relationship, and we had a lot of other people praying for us too."

Joseph nods in agreement.

"When I attend a wedding, I worry for those couples who stand up there with smug smiles on their faces," he says. "As far as I'm concerned, I'd rather see a clear-eyed man and woman whose faces are full of humble hope."

> *O LORD, You have heard the desire of the humble; You will strengthen their heart.*
>
> PSALM 10:17 NASB

To love is to be vulnerable.

C. S. LEWIS

42

Take a "chemistry" class.

Moriah and Benny Trujillo

MARRIED MAY 29, 1956

Moriah Trujillo had options when it came to romance. She was the 1950s epitome of a "hottie." Many young men desired her company. But she knew Benny was her one and only, and the choice wasn't that difficult for her. It wasn't that the young Mr. Trujillo was the richest guy in town, the most dashing, or the most athletic. But he had one important trait that set him apart from all of the other suitors in the greater Salem, Oregon, area.

"Benny was the *only* one who didn't irritate me," Moriah remembers. "He and I just clicked. There was something about his personality—his whole nature—that was a perfect fit for me. With everyone else, there was something about the way they talked to me or carried themselves that simply rubbed me the wrong way. Around Benny, though, my nerves were at peace. He has always been a class guy."

Moriah's advice for young lovers?

"Don't focus on who looks good—or who you think makes *you* look good," she says. "Go for the person you truly enjoy just being around. Because that's what marriage is—a lot of two people being around each other. And if you don't have the right chemistry, something's gonna blow up."

Benny nods in agreement.

"You young people: If you're going to major in something," he says, "major in chemistry. If you know what I mean…"

> *But encourage one another day after*
> *day, as long as it is still called "Today."*
>
> HEBREWS 3:13 NASB

Love is friendship set to music.

JACKSON POLLOCK

43

You gotta keep dancin'.

Joshua and Elizabeth Hartman
MARRIED MAY 12, 1954

Many happily married couples have a hobby or pastime they enjoy sharing. For the Hartmans, it's dancing.

"We've always enjoyed dancing," Joshua says, "ever since I tricked her into marrying me, back in Omaha, Nebraska, in the good old days. I just hoped that by the time she found out what I was really like, enough time would have passed so that she'd figure she was stuck with me."

"Actually, I tricked *you* into marrying *me*," Elizabeth corrects her husband. "But you're right about the dancing. It was fun, and it helped me start liking you pretty good—around year forty-five or so into the marriage."

The frequency of the activity has changed, but the Hartmans still enjoy dancing together, after almost sixty years of marriage.

"Of course I still dance with her," Joshua laughs. "Just look at her, will you? I dance with that pretty wife of mine every chance I get. In fact, somebody put on some music!"

Let them praise His name
with dancing; Let them
sing praises to Him.

PSALM 149:3 NASB

*W*hat love requires, on top of instant emotion, is time, shared experiences and feelings, and a long, tempered bond between two people.

STANTON PEELE

44

Encourage—don't nag.

Doug and Marie Larson

MARRIED APRIL 30, 1957

A strong marriage gives each partner the security and freedom to help one's spouse grow and improve as a person. There is a fine line, however, between encouragement and nagging. Doug and Marie Larson say that 55 years of marriage have given them a keen sense of exactly where that line is.

"You cannot be petty about things," Marie explains, "but a husband and wife can really help each other improve—in ways large and small. For example, I noticed that Doug, who is very shy, struggled to look people in the eyes during a conversation. I pointed out this tendency to him, gently noting that some people might assume he was aloof, or even dishonest.

"He understood and improved his eye contact right away. He 'backslides' sometimes, but it seems to help when I remind him of what beautiful blue eyes he has.

"As for me, I had a tendency to talk with my mouth full of food. I am very manners-conscious, mind you, but this was a total blind spot of mine. I am sure lots of people noticed, but Doug was the only one comfortable with pointing this out to me. Now I do a better job of keeping my yap shut if I'm working on a burger or something."

"If a husband and wife continually affirm each other," Doug adds (looking his interviewer squarely in the eyes), "it gives you permission to gently note ways you can help each other grow. Marie and I are better people, in large and small ways, because of how we have encouraged each other over the years. I don't know what I would have done without her. But it would have probably included wandering through life with my eyes downcast...and my fly open to boot."

If your gift is to encourage others, be encouraging. If it is giving, give generously.

ROMANS 12:8 NLT

I love you because you
Are helping me to make...
Out of the works
Of my every day
Not a reproach
But a song.

ROY CROFT

45

Believe in the power of God's peace.

Marsh and Elaine Gabriel

MARRIED JULY 24, 1949

In 1968, Marsh Gabriel decided to sell his printing business to give something else a try. He became a sea captain, just as he had been decades earlier, in World War II. Meanwhile, Elaine stayed home, faithfully raising their four sons and one daughter. Elaine recalls the night that Marsh returned to the sea. The family enjoyed a celebrative send-off, and then Marsh flew to his port. Elaine and the children somberly returned home. She went to bed, crying miserably.

To make matters worse, while alone in her room Elaine felt gripped by an overwhelming cold terror as she considered what it meant to take on the daily responsibilities of both a mom and a dad. She looked at a nearby clock. It was almost 2:00 a.m., too late to call even a close friend. So she cried out to God in prayer. She recited verses from the Bible. Suddenly and mysteriously, the words of Isaiah 26:3 spoke powerfully to her: "You will keep in perfect peace those whose minds are steadfast, because they trust in you."

Moments later, Elaine experienced what she can only describe as a miracle. "An incredible peace washed over me," she recalls. "A peace that surprised me—and actually caused me to laugh."

The Gabriels' situation had not changed, of course. But Elaine says that God changed her heart that night.

"His peace calmed my soul and my mind," she says. "And that palpable terror never returned during all the difficult years that Marsh was at sea."

Years later, Marsh and Elaine would need that powerful peace of God, when their 15-year-old son, Brian, was paralyzed from the neck down in a diving accident. Marsh was summoned from his ship to the hospital—where he and Elaine were told that Brian would probably never regain the use of his arms and legs. The two parents were incredibly saddened, but also surprised by an inexplicable sense of peace—even as they received the heart-breaking prognosis.

"Once again," Elaine reports, "God's peace rushed into the room and reminded us that no matter what the circumstances might be, He was in control."

Marsh and Elaine assert that in the midst of huge challenges, and even tragic circumstances, God's peace—which surpasses all logic and comprehension—will not let them down.

Elaine says, "It is God's peace that holds us. God and His Word."

Sometimes, God heals those he holds. To the shock of his physicians, Brian Gabriel *did* eventually walk again. He is currently employed as a sea captain. Just like his dad.

"You will keep in perfect peace
those whose minds are steadfast,
because they trust in you.

ISAIAH 26:3

*L*ove—thoughts of tenderness,
tried in temptation, strengthened by
distress, unmoved by absence, and
yet, more than all, untired by time.

LORD BYRON

True Love Trivia

Stay-at-home dad Michael Thompson's wife
was content to let her husband mind the kids
while she worked. However, Thompson ended
up making a huge financial contribution to
the family one memorable year. He won
one million dollars in a fantasy-fishing contest.

46

Try a little kindness.

A.J. and Ann Jefferson

MARRIED JULY 18, 1946

It started with an eye-roll from Ann's sister, Sue.

"A.J. and I had been married about a year, and I was 'asking' him to do an errand for me," Ann recalls. "And by asking, I mean…*nagging*.

"Sue, who was over for a visit, gave me this look. Then she said, 'Are you *always* this much of a grump to him? You didn't even say *please*.'

"I got defensive. I said something like, 'Hey—he talks to me the same way. Besides, what business is it of yours?'

"Then Sue gave me the look again. 'Well then,' she said, 'I feel sorry for both of you.' Those words really knocked me sideways. We were still newlyweds, really, and we were already taking each other for granted. We were not even showing the common courtesy we'd give to a complete stranger. Even to a door-to-door salesman!"

And so the Jeffersons started paying closer attention to their inter-actions. They were shocked at how much sarcasm, indifference, and, sometimes, downright rudeness had crept into their communication. They made a vow to show each other more kindness, more grace, and more love.

"It makes a world of difference when Ann asks me for something in a voice that's sweet and polite," A.J. says. "And I know she appreciates it when I don't get all bent out of shape when she asks me to repeat some-thing I just said. It's ironic, you know: Sometimes your own spouse is the last person you'll show a little kindness to. He or she should be the first."

Serve one another humbly in love.

GALATIANS 5:13

When we hurt each other, we
should write it down in the sand,
so the winds of forgiveness can
make it go away for good. When we
help each other, we should chisel
it in stone, lest we never forget.

CHRISTIAN H. GODEFROY

47

Don't just be lovers; be friends.

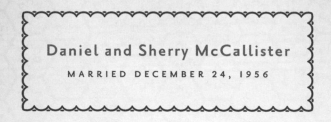

Daniel and Sherry McCallister

MARRIED DECEMBER 24, 1956

Talk to a few longtime happily married couples, and you're likely to hear comments like, "I married my best friend."

Count the McCallisters among this friendly bunch. For Daniel and Sherry, their union didn't grow out of a need for financial security, social status, or physical romance.

As Daniel puts it, simply, "I needed a friend, and that is what I found in Sherry. That's what she found in me. For us, the romantic love stuff was just the cherry on top. It's been that way ever since our Christmas Eve wedding. She's the best Christmas present I could have hoped for."

Marrying out of friendship might not sound romantic—the stuff of movies and epic love poems. But it works. As the McCallisters are quick to point out, when you're struggling with your career or facing major self-esteem issues, a candlelight dinner, box of fancy chocolates, or vase of a dozen roses probably won't help all that much. Those are the times when one needs a caring and sympathetic ear—and some wise friend-to-friend counsel.

"The Bible says that 'a friend loves at all times,'" Sherry notes. "And when times are tough, the *last* thing I need is violin music, incense, and mood lighting. I need my best friend, and that's Daniel. I know he feels the same way about me."

> *So this is my prayer: that your love will flourish*
> *and that you will not only love much but well....*
> *You need to use your head and test your feelings*
> *so that your love is sincere and intelligent,*
> *not sentimental gush. Live a lover's life.*
>
> PHILIPPIANS 1:9–10 MSG

*S*exiness wears thin after a while and beauty fades, but to be married to a man who makes you laugh every day, ah, now that's a real treat.

JOANNE WOODWARD

48

Don't go to bed angry.

William and Wendy Collins
MARRIED APRIL 21, 1951

At their wedding, the minister instructed William and Wendy Collins, "Do not go to bed angry." It seemed like reasonable advice at the time. But once the stresses of marriage began to wear down the twosome, that wedding-day mandate seemed impossible to follow.

In the heat of battle, they found that trying to follow the minister's advice actually made things worse. On top of everything else, they felt pressure to, in William's words, "settle this stupid argument before bedtime!"

Frustrated, William and Wendy returned to their minister. He listened patiently as the couple accused him of giving them an impossible mission.

Then he spoke gently.

"Think back to what I said—*exactly* what I said," the pastor said. "I didn't say that you had to solve every argument and feel completely at peace about everything—all before 10 p.m."

"Yes, you did!" William snapped. "You can ask my best man—or anyone who was paying attention to what you said. We might even still have it recorded on the reel-to-reel!"

"No," the pastor replied. "I merely said to avoid going to bed *angry*. You don't have to solve your problem before you turn off the lights. You don't even have to feel great about each other. You just need to find a way to let the anger dissipate. That might mean calling a temporary truce. Or taking a long walk to cool off before turning in."

That conversation was a revelation to William and Wendy.

"We'd been putting all this pressure on ourselves," Wendy recalls, "to solve every problem and find perfect bliss—or we weren't allowed to go to sleep. All we really needed to do was make sure we didn't hit the pillows with hearts and heads full of anger and resentment. Now, mind you, that in itself is not easy, but at least it is do-able. And if you avoid going to bed angry, the problems are so much easier to deal with when the morning comes."

May the Lord make your love
increase and overflow for each
other and for everyone else.

I THESSALONIANS 3:12

*W*e are most alive when we're in love.

JOHN UPDIKE

49

If you must fight, fight fair.

Dean and Lynn Larson

MARRIED JUNE 6, 1953

"You can't be in close quarters with someone for half a century and not step on each other's nerves once in a while," Lynn Larson observes. "I hear these couples who say, 'We never had one argument in fifty years,' and I wonder what drugs they have been on. Let's be real here: If you're passionate about your relationship—and passionate about each other—the sparks are gonna fly sometimes."

The Larsons contend that conflict can actually be constructive—if it's handled maturely and prayerfully. After a few heated arguments early in their marriage, they began to work on a list of rules for a Fair Fight.

Today, that time-tested Larson List reads like this:

- Focus on the problem, not the person. Don't get cruel or personal. (It's okay to say, "You didn't mow the lawn as you promised you would." This, however, is NOT okay: "You're an unreliable, lazy slob.")

• Focus on the issue at hand. No fair bringing up past grievances. (This is a biggie.)

• Listen. Listen some more.

• Affirm your partner and your love for him or her. It's so important to do this in times of conflict.

• Take some time to cool down, if needed. (Talk a long walk. Listen to some music. Pray. Breathe.)

• Don't be too proud to call upon a referee if needed. (The referee might be a counselor, psychologist, religious leader, or, as Lynn notes, "God Almighty Himself.")

• Did we mention, LISTEN?

"Because we've insisted on our fights being fair," Lynn says, "our marriage has been better than fair. It's been excellent!"

Dean chuckles, "There's no fightin' that conclusion, baby!"

A light shines in the dark for honest people, for those who are merciful and kind and good.

PSALM 112:4 NCV

*T*he ultimate test of a relationship is
to disagree but to hold hands.

ALEXANDRA PENNEY

50

Give each other room to grow.

Mark and Pam Cooper
MARRIED APRIL 21, 1951

According to Pam and Mark Cooper, marriage gives a couple a choice when it comes to change and personal growth.

"You can marry someone," Pam explains, "and then try to spend the rest of your married life trying to change him or her into someone else. Or you can allow the one you married to grow his or her own way—without a bunch of meddling or manipulation. Instead of criticism, you provide space, nurturing, and prayer. Lots and lots of prayer."

"There's a world of difference between those two options," Mark adds.

"From day one," Pam says, "I accepted Mark for who he was. But that didn't mean I didn't want the best for him and from him. I prayed for that all of the time."

Meanwhile, a decade into their marriage, Mark found himself stressed out and creatively stifled in his career as a salesperson. It affected his health and his marriage. He wanted to go back to school and earn his teaching credentials. At first, he hesitated sharing his thoughts with Pam. After all, their income would be cut almost in half if he followed through with his plan. But one night, in frustration, Mark spilled the contents of his heart.

Pam asked a few questions. Then she threw her full support behind her husband.

"It was the best thing for him," she explains, "and in the long run, it was the best thing for us."

YOU CAN MARRY SOMEONE AND THEN TRY
TO SPEND THE REST OF YOUR MARRIED LIFE
TRYING TO CHANGE THEM. OR YOU CAN
ALLOW THEM TO GROW THEIR WAY.

She helped Mark choose a school where he could earn his teaching certification. She also increased her hours at the office where she worked as a bookkeeper.

A few years later, when Pam became a serious runner, Mark had the opportunity to return the favor, as he trained with her, supported her at races, and shouldered a larger share of the household duties while she was training for major events such as triathlons and marathons.

"Like a lot of couples, our marriage vows talked about 'for better,'" Mark says, "and to us that concept transcends circumstances. It means helping each other be *better people*, helping each other reach personal and professional goals."

"People change in different ways, and at different paces," Pam says. "You never know how God is going to mold a life. But the result can be beautiful if people will just get out of His way! If God is leading your spouse down a new road, you shouldn't be creating speed bumps. You should be getting rid of them."

*For we are his workmanship, created
in Christ Jesus for good works,
which God prepared beforehand
so that we would walk in them.*

EPHESIANS 2:10 NASB

Your marriage is a living poem. Some marriages are sonnets; some are haiku. But each marriage is a unique work of art. As a living poem, your marriage is being written one day at a time— as woman, man, and God hold the pen.

VICKI KUYPER

True Love Trivia

Alexander Graham Bell did not set out to
invent the telephone. It was an unintended
side product, springing from the 29-year-old
inventor's efforts to create a device to
help his wife and his mom, who were both
deaf, to hear and communicate better.

51

Listen to what's <u>not</u> being said.

QUINTON AND TOGI BARELA

MARRIED FEBRUARY 14, 1954

The Barelas urge all couples to "come to their senses." But for this couple, the advice isn't what it seems at face value. Quinton and Togi, who were married in Hawaii on Valentine's Day, find it odd that many men and women don't use *all* of their senses in marriage. Including the senses that transcend the physical.

"You don't necessarily need to hear words to understand what your spouse is thinking or feeling," Quinton says. "In fact, you shouldn't rely just on words."

The Barelas have become experts in picking up on non-verbal cues—a knowing smile, a downcast face, a sluggish gait, a sense of tension or apprehension in the bedroom. A clinging hug that says, "I really need your support and love right now!" A slight quake in one's voice—a cry of, "I'm trying to hold it together, but I'm hurt. And I'm scared."

Quinton and Togi know that when it comes to understanding your spouse and responding to his or her needs, what's *not* said is often more significant than what *is* said.

And, similarly, the context of a sentence or two sometimes outshines the words themselves.

"Words are fine," Togi says, "but when you are truly tuned in to your partner, you'll find that, quite often, you don't even need words to understand each other. You are in touch with each other's spirit. And that's a beautiful thing."

Blessed the man, blessed the woman, who listens to me, awake and ready for me each morning, alert and responsive as I start my day's work.

PROVERBS 8:34 MSG

*F*ew delights can equal the mere presence of one whom we trust utterly.

GEORGE MACDONALD

52

Pick your battles, <u>carefully</u>.

Finances. Household chores. Job-related pressures. Kid-related pressures. Bickering in-laws. Health challenges. Division of labor. The list of stressors to a marriage could fill a book.

Combine big problems like the ones above with a few minor annoyances—a partner's snoring, a to-do list that never gets to-done—and the average married couple can find enough fuel to keep them bickering 24/7, month after month.

The Kralls fully realized this truth about two years into their marriage when they came to the end of a three-day weekend and realized they had spent virtually every waking hour complaining, kvetching, or commiserating about one thing or another.

"We realized we had just wasted a whole long weekend," Marie remembers. "And so the question came: 'Just how much of our married life do we want to throw away by bickering?' I mean, seriously, there's some stuff you simply must let go."

Gene adds, "Neither one of us likes to argue. But back in the day, you'd think we were both *itching* for a fight. Go figure…"

Obviously, major issues cannot—and should not—be avoided, but the Kralls learned that there is wisdom in showing one another a little grace once in a while.

"Just because you *could* have a dust-up about something," Marie asserts, "doesn't mean you *should*!"

Today, with her husband now passed on, Marie says she is glad their 51-year marriage wasn't marred by constant "fussing and fighting."

"I miss Gene every day," Marie says, "but I'm glad that I'm living with so many happy memories instead of regrets over silly fights that, in the big picture, didn't matter at all."

Be kind and compassionate to one another, forgiving each other, just as in Christ God forgave you.

EPHESIANS 4:32

To keep your marriage brimming
With love in the loving cup,
Whenever you're wrong, admit it;
Whenever you're right, shut up.

OGDEN NASH

53

Enjoy the simple things in life.

ROY AND FAY BLACK

MARRIED FEBRUARY 28, 1943

Between the two of them, Roy and Fay Black didn't have a car when they were married. They caught a ride with Roy's best man to their wedding. Roy took the bus to work every day.

"I was a bit hamstrung when it came to taking my new bride out for a date," Roy says. "With no car, we weren't going very far."

But sometimes romance can spring from humble circumstances. Several times a week, the Blacks embarked on walking dates, visiting the park near their apartment or strolling through the neighborhood and enjoying the sights—always hand in hand.

"We saw sunsets, children playing, red-tailed hawks soaring, and wispy clouds passing in front of plump full moons," Fay remembers. "I'll take that over any movie, play, or restaurant. "

Roy and Fay have his-and-hers cars these days, but they still enjoy leaving the vehicles in the garage and venturing out on foot.

"The sunsets are just as beautiful as ever," Roy says. "And so is Fay."

"Therefore be imitators of God, as beloved children; and walk in love, just as Christ also loved you and gave Himself up for us.

EPHESIANS 5:1–2 NASB

*L*ove will grow as reasons for love are discovered, thought about, dwelt upon in the mind, expressed verbally, and remembered. As time goes on, the memory will become rich with increasing vividness and warmth.

EDITH SCHAEFFER

Two Couples on the Road to Gold

Just before *Forever Love* went to press, two couples edged their way into my heart—and onto the book's pages.

Marv and Marcia Edwards began work on year 49 of their marriage. Meanwhile, Mike Whim Jr. and Katy Wild announced their engagement. (As you read these words, they are probably picking rice grains out of one another's hair.)

It seems fitting, then, to end this book with two more love stories, one almost half a century old and the other just beginning.

There's no ability like responsibility.

Although their golden anniversary is in clear sight, Marcia and Marv Edwards look toward their milestone with the same humility, caution, and tempered hope that have guided their lives.

"We'll probably just have a small celebration at our church," says Marcia, a retired elementary school teacher. "And we want to pay for everything, just like we did with our wedding."

Marv and Marcia were 28 and 27, respectively, when they married in 1964, several years older than most of their peers. "When we got engaged," Marcia recalls, "my dad told me, 'Prepare for poverty!' But we were determined to avoid that. We had been dating for two years, and we were both working. In fact, I had already been teaching for five years when we got married."

Marv, meanwhile, worked underground—literally—at Dow Chemical, in a high-security capacity serving the military.

An avid fisherman hailing from Coffeyville, Kansas, he was much happier when he moved up, in many senses of the word, to a job with the Colorado Department of Wildlife. He also became a regular contributing writer to *Colorado Outdoor Magazine*.

. . . .

IN THEIR QUIET AND MEASURED WAY,
THEY HAVE BECOME EXEMPLARS OF JUST
HOW NOBLE A MARRIAGE CAN BE.

. . . .

"Marv and I have lived on a dual income most of our life," Marcia says. However, she is quick to point out that her salary was ignored when it came to qualifying for a home loan in 1965. "Even though I actually made more money than Marv," she says, "my salary didn't count in qualifying for a mortgage—unless I could provide a doctor's confirmation that I was unable to bear children."

Parenthood was part of the couple's plans, so they were thankful when Marv's salary was deemed adequate to cover the monthly house payment of $125 dollars a month. They moved into a modest brick home in a Denver, Colorado suburb, where they still live today.

"We've always tried to be responsible about things," Marcia says. "When we had our daughter, Abby, we had saved enough to replace my salary while I took time to stay at home and care for her before resuming teaching.

Marcia notes that her maternity leave wasn't optional. "Our school district's policy was that all pregnant teachers had to leave by their fourth month. Some of us asked if we could stay and teach longer. The principal told us, 'Let's see how you feel.' That was code for, 'Let's see how you *look*.' For some reason, the administration did not want an obviously pregnant woman standing up in front of a class."

All told, Marcia taught for forty-three years. "I was at it so long that some of my first students are now retired," she says. "Talk about making you feel old!"

Marv and Marcia's measured approach to life has served them well in recent years. Three years ago, Marcia's health took a severe hit. She has lived with uncertainty and chronic pain as various doctors have hurled various diagnoses and treatments at her, like children throwing different-size pebbles from a gravel driveway—hoping something will hit the target.

I'VE SEEN THEM REMAIN FAITHFUL TO EACH OTHER IN WORD AND DEED WHEN IT WOULD HAVE BEEN EASY TO THROW IN THE TOWEL.

Through it all, Marv and Marcia have remained active in their church, while also supporting their three grandchildren in their various athletic and artistic endeavors. Marv has become a caregiver par excellence. He's spent much of the past three years in hospitals and emergency wards, a sad irony for a man who's never been hospitalized in his life. (He was even born at home.)

In their quiet and measured way, Marv and Marcia have become exemplars of just how noble a marriage can be.

"I am continually amazed at my parents' commitment to each other through many ups and downs over the years," says their daughter, Abby Lopez. "I've seen them remain faithful to each other in word and deed when it would have been easy to throw in the towel. The true test of their love has definitely been in the past three years—with Mom's illness and frequent pain. Dad has selflessly given his all to try to help Mom cope with this enormous hardship. I've seen a side of my dad that I'd never seen before. He has taken over the household duties and devoted endless hours to caring for Mom's physical needs.

"For her part, I have seen my mom demonstrate a sweet and gracious spirit in the midst of great struggle. I am truly inspired by both of my parents!"

She is not the only one. When Marv and Marcia celebrate their golden anniversary, friends and relatives from hundreds of miles away plan to be present. And they say they will do their best to prevent the Edwardses from paying for their own celebration this time around.

Sing a new song to the LORD,
for he has done wonderful deeds.
His right hand has won a mighty victory;
His holy arm has shown his saving power!

PSALM 98:1 NLT

*A*ll that we love deeply
becomes a part of us.

HELEN KELLER

Forever Love

Love. No greater theme can be
emphasized. No stronger message can be
proclaimed. No finer song can be sung.
No better truth can be imagined.

CHARLES R. SWINDOLL

*Love is
friendship on fire.*

Katy Wild and her fiancé, Mike Whim Jr., saw their romance take its opening bow on that legendary love stage: church puppet ministry.

"My mom was talking about her church's puppetry program," Mike recalls, "and she happened to mention that I should visit her church soon. She told me that one of the puppeteers was 'a really cute girl.'"

Mike was intrigued, but skeptical. "Mom," I told her, "I've helped out with church puppet ministries before. There is *no* such thing as a cute girl in church puppet ministry."

And then Mike met Katy.

"What can I say?" he confesses. "I was wrong. She's hot."

Mike knows all about *hot*. He is a firefighter/EMT.

Katy's first impression of Mike was favorable too—although less…
guy-like.

"He seemed like a nice guy," she recalls. "He had a nice handshake."

Handshakes turned to hugs. Before long, Mike and Katy were partners
in the puppet ministry, with plans to be partners in life as well.

The engaged duo took time out from wedding planning, college studies
(Katy is pursuing her Masters degree in Library Science), and fighting
fires and providing emergency medical care to answer a few questions
about a young love that they believe will go the distance.

Q: *You dated for a year and a half before becoming engaged—how
long did it take to realize your relationship was special?*

Mike: I had this rule in my head: Wait a year before making a
serious commitment. I stuck to my rule. We dated 18 months
before we got engaged. But it only took about three months
for me to know I'd found the one.

Katy: For *both* of us to know.

Q: *As an engaged couple, what's your take on today's high
divorce rate?*

Mike: My parents went through a divorce, and that has definitely influenced how I look at marriage. It has made me
very determined. I take the marriage vows very seriously.
When I say my vows, I will be making promises. Promises
that I will keep. Katy and I will build our marriage on a

strong Christian foundation. We're coming into it with that perspective. We are going to work together to make a strong marriage.

Katy: I am thankful that we are both coming into marriage with the same values. We have a similar perspective on life, love, and faith.

Q: *Are children part of your future plans?*

Katy: Definitely. Right?

Mike: Yes ma'am.

Q: *What kind of parents do you hope to be?*

Mike: I want to let my kids get out and explore life. But I also know that I will need to put the hammer down sometimes.

Katy: I want to encourage their critical-thinking skills. Especially when it comes to faith. I want them to really *think* about their faith. Mike and I will help them work through their challenges, but, in the end, their decisions will be their own. You have to develop your own faith, not have it spoon-fed to you.

Also, I hope I will be a patient parent.

Q: *Let's fast-forward to the day you two are celebrating your golden wedding anniversary: What will be the hallmarks of your marriage?*

Katy: I hope Mike and I will be able to say that we were true to ourselves and our faith. We didn't let anything change the core of who we are, both as individuals and as a married couple.

Mike: I hope people will look at us and say, "That is a marriage that has been lived through Christ." That's what I want our kids—and everyone else—to see.

We know that God causes everything
to work together for the good of
those who love God and are called
according to his purpose for them.

ROMANS 8:28 NLT

*S*ince love grows within you, so beauty grows. For love is the beauty of the soul.

ST. AUGUSTINE

ACKNOWLEDGMENTS

Thank you, Bonnie Sparrman, for the stories of Paul and Gunnie Sparrman and Marsh and Elaine Gabriel.

Thank you, T.J. Hafer, for the story of Larry and Freda Brink, and for your editing expertise.

Thank you, Marcia Edwards and Jerry Springston, for all of your help with the story of Jim and Neva Springston.

Thank you, Abby Lopez, for your heartfelt insights into your parents' marriage.

Thank you, Scott Degelman and Jedd Hafer, for your diligent research.

A final word of thanks to the people at Regal Books and to Ron Hafer for the background information and insights on John Wooden.

*Editor's Note: It's appropriate that a book about a love that endures for years took years to research, compile, and edit. In most cases, we were able to talk with both members of each of the couples featured in these pages. However, at times, we relied on the recollections of a surviving member of a couple, a couple's children and close friends, and/or books, journals, and diaries that were made available to us.

Also, in rare instances we encountered a couple eager to share their story but wary of revealing their full names or other identifying biographical information. This reluctance was due to concerns about identity theft, which, sadly, had victimized them in the past. To respect these couples' privacy, we have used only the first letter of their last name (or a fictitious surname) and been intentionally vague about background information.